My Aha Moments With God

All rights reserved.

No part of this publication may be reproduced, distributed, or transmitted in any form or by any means, including photocopying, recording, or other electronic or mechanical methods, without the prior written permission of the publisher, except in the case of brief quotations embodied in critical reviews and certain other noncommercial uses permitted by copyright law.

All scripture quotations are taken from the King James Version. Public Domain.

# MY AHA MOMENTS WITH GOD

Karen Rutherford

All scripture quotations are taken from the Holy Bible, King James Version (Public Domain)

To my parents, Bishop Robert Simpson, Jr.
and Dr. Ida M. Simpson -
*For always loving me and raising me to wholeheartedly serve God. Rest in peace. I love you and will remember you always!*


To my family -
*For your support and letting me be uniquely me. Thanks. I love you all!*


To my pastor, Pastor T. Renea Glenn –
*For lovingly feeding me with knowledge and understanding and always sharing the heart of the Father. I'm all in! I love you. Thank you!*

# INTRODUCTION

In My Aha Moments With God, I share with you excerpts of my conversations with God, at various times during my Christian journey. I pray that you will be as enlightened as I have been, and inspired to pursue God as never before!

# God is the only One who truly satisfies!

*For he satisfieth the longing soul, and filleth the hungry soul with goodness.*
Psalm 107:9

*Reflections -*

# Excited about the future, yet content in the present.

*Not that I speak in respect of want: for I have learned, in whatsoever state I am, therewith to be content.*
Philippians 4:11

*Reflections -*

# Just resting in Jesus; trusting His plan and process – that's where I am.

*For I know the thoughts that I think toward you, saith the LORD, thoughts of peace, and not of evil, to give you an expected end.*
Jeremiah 29:11

*Reflections -*

# Called and chosen out of so many to be a part of the Kingdom of God, what an honor and a privilege!

*But ye are a chosen generation a royal priesthood, an holy nation, a peculiar people; that ye should shew forth the praises of him who called you out of darkness into his marvellous light: Which in time past were not a people, but are now the people of God: which had not obtained mercy, but now have obtained mercy.*
1 Peter 2:9-10

*Reflections -*

# God's secret place is beyond words, beyond explaining. One must just experience it, to know it!

*He that dwelleth in the secret place of the most High shall abide under the shadow of the Almighty.*
Psalm 91:1

*Reflections -*

# Sitting in the presence of God, I realize even more, that I never want to be without Him.

*One thing have I desired of the LORD, that will I seek after; that I may dwell in the house of the LORD all the days of my life, to behold the beauty of the LORD, and to enquire in his temple.*
Psalm 27:4

*Reflections -*

**My life, now, is the result of my prayer of relinquishment of life…I have turned over to God, the right to determine the course of my life.**

*O Lord, I know that the way of man is not in himself:*
*it is not in man that walketh to direct his steps.*
Jeremiah 10:23

*Reflections -*

# God, undergird me as I press on the upward way!

*I press toward the mark for the prize of the high calling of God in Christ Jesus.*
Philippians 3:14

*Reflections -*

**There is truly no love like God's love –
so encompassing, fulfilling, satisfying,
and unconditional. God's love is bold,
yet gentle; strong and uplifting.
I never want to live without Him.**

*The LORD hath appeared of old unto me, saying, Yea, I have
loved thee with an everlasting love: therefore with
lovingkindness have I drawn thee.*
Jeremiah 31:3

*But God commendeth his love toward us, in that, while we were
yet sinners, Christ died for us.*
Romans 5:8

*Reflections -*

# God, I'd be so lost without You!

*For in him we live, and move, and have our being;*
Acts 17:28a

# Where I was then and where I am now are a million light years apart!

*Therefore if any man be in Christ, he is a new creature: old things are passed away; behold, all things are become new.*
2 Corinthians 5:17

# How precious are the lessons in life that build faith in God!

*That the trial of your faith, being much more precious than of gold that perisheth, though it be tried with fire, might be found unto praise and honour and glory at the appearing of Jesus Christ: Whom having not seen, ye love; in whom, though now ye see him not, yet believing, ye rejoice with joy unspeakable and full of glory: Receiving the end of your faith, even the salvation of your souls.*
1 Peter 1:7-9

*Reflections -*

God, I'll never forget the work You performed in me and on me. I have further to go, but I'm grateful from whence I have come.

*Being confident of this very thing that he which hath begun a good work in you will perform it until the day of Jesus Christ.*
Philippians 1:6

Reflections -

# God, I never thought that I would know You as I do.

*And this is life eternal, that they might know thee the only true God, and Jesus Christ, whom thou hast sent.*
John 17:3

*Reflections -*

**Thank You, Lord, for the grace to make it through the journey of life: the struggles, the victories, the challenges, the disappointments, the joys, and the sorrows. I realize and acknowledge that it's Your faithfulness, grace, and mercy that carry me through it all.**

*When thou passest through the waters, I will be with thee; and through the rivers, they shall not overflow thee: when thou walkest through the fire, thou shalt not be burned; neither shall the flame kindle upon thee.*
Isaiah 43:2

*Reflections -*

*Reflections -*

**Thank You for Your mercy that kept me, when I should have been cut off. God, I am amazed at the wonders of Your grace.**

*It is of the LORD's mercies that we are not consumed, because his compassions fail not.*
*They are new every morning: great is thy faithfulness.*
Lamentations 3:22-23

*Reflections -*

# There are so many things that I am grateful for today!

*Bless the Lord, O my soul, and forget not all his benefits: Who forgiveth all thine iniquities; who healeth all thy diseases; Who redeemeth thy life from destruction; who crowneth thee with lovingkindness and tender mercies; Who satisfieth thy mouth with good things; so that thy youth is renewed like the eagle's.*
Psalm 103:2-5

*Reflections -*

I had a glimpse of my life without You and it scared me. The look of sin, the life of sin is not for me. I choose You, Lord, again and again.

*One thing have I desired of the LORD, that will I seek after; that I may dwell in the house of the LORD all the days of my life, to behold the beauty of the LORD, and to enquire in his temple.*
Psalm 27:4

*Reflections -*

# I never want to fail You again.

*Who can understand his errors? cleanse thou me from secret faults. Keep back thy servant also from presumptuous sins; let them not have dominion over me: then shall I be upright, and I shall be innocent from the great transgression.*
*Psalm 19:12-13*

*Reflections -*

# Lord, thank You for the strength to take the way of escape!

*There hath no temptation taken you but such as is common to man: but God is faithful, who will not suffer you to be tempted above that ye are able; but will with the temptation also make a way to escape, that ye may be able to bear it.*
1 Corinthians 10:13

*Reflections -*

# Thank You for guarding my life!

*He that dwelleth in the secret place of the most High shall abide under the shadow of the Almighty. I will say of the LORD, He is my refuge and my fortress: my God; in him will I trust. Surely he shall deliver thee from the snare of the fowler, and from the noisome pestilence. He shall cover thee with his feathers, and under his wings shalt thou trust: his truth shall be thy shield and buckler. Thou shalt not be afraid for the terror by night; nor for the arrow that flieth by day; Nor for the pestilence that walketh in darkness; nor for the destruction that wasteth at noonday. A thousand shall fall at thy side, and ten thousand at thy right hand; but it shall not come nigh thee. Only with thine eyes shalt thou behold and see the reward of the wicked. Because thou hast made the LORD, which is my refuge, even the most High, thy habitation; There shall no evil befall thee, neither shall any plague come nigh thy dwelling. For he shall give his angels charge over thee, to keep thee in all thy ways. They shall bear thee up in their hands, lest thou dash thy foot against a stone. Thou shalt tread upon the lion and adder: the young lion and the dragon shalt thou trample under feet. Because he hath set his love upon me, therefore will I deliver him: I will set him on high, because he hath known my name. He shall call upon me, and I will answer him: I will be with him in trouble; I will deliver him and honour him. With long life will I satisfy him, and shew him my salvation.*

Psalm 91:1-16

*Reflections -*

# When things get crazy and the waters of life get murky, I thank God that He remains in control.

*Fear thou not; for I am with thee: be not dismayed; for I am thy God: I will strengthen thee; yea, I will help thee; yea, I will uphold thee with the right hand of my righteousness.*
Isaiah 41:10

*Reflections -*

**God, I never have to question Your motives, Your intentions, Your way or Your actions…all that You do is good! There is never a danger zone with You, I never have to wonder!**

*The LORD is righteous in all his ways, and holy in all his works.*
Psalm 145:17

*Reflections -*

**The state in which You found me was unfixable by human means. I was damaged, broken and without hope of recovery. But You, God, took me and made something beautiful out of my life.**

*Then they cried unto the LORD in their trouble, and he saved them out of their distresses. He brought then out of darkness and the shadow of death, and brake their bands in sunder. Oh that men would praise the LORD for his goodness, and for his wonderful works to the children of men! For he hath broken the gates of brass, and cut the bars of iron in sunder.*
Psalm 107:13-16


*But he was wounded for our transgressions, he was bruised for our iniquities: the chastisement of our peace was upon him: and with his stripes we are healed.*
Isaiah 53:5

**Oh, to be kept by God…is such a wonderful thing. It feels so good to know that You are with me – ordering my steps, leading, and guiding me. I don't know what I would do, if I had to navigate through this life all by myself.
Just the thought is overwhelming!**

*My soul, wait thou only upon God; for my expectation is from him. He only is my rock and my salvation: he is my defence; I shall not be moved. In God is my salvation and my glory: the rock of my strength, and my refuge, is in God. Trust in him at all times; ye people, pour out your heart before him: God is a refuge for us.*
Psalm 62:5-8

*Reflections -*

**God's agenda is so easy to follow. Love Him with all of our hearts, acknowledge Him in all our ways, and obey His commandments written in the Holy Bible. But too often, we complicate God's agenda by analyzing it and attempting to alter it. If we, the children of God would simply go where God leads and eat what God feeds, our success is guaranteed.**

*Trust in the LORD with all thine heart; and lean not unto thine own understanding. In all thy ways acknowledge him, and he shall direct thy paths. Be not wise in thine own eyes: fear the LORD, and depart from evil. It shall be health to thy navel, and marrow to thy bones. Honour the LORD with thy substance, and with the firstfruits of thine increase: So shall thy barns be filled with plenty, and thy presses shall burst out with new wine. My son, despise not the chastening of the LORD; neither be weary of his correction: For who the LORD loveth he correcteth; even as a father the son in whom he delighteth. Happy is the man that findeth wisdom, and the man that getteth understanding.*
Proverbs 3:5-13

# Distractions, diversions, hindrances and turmoil – all a part of satan's scheme to cause the saints to lose focus. In times of spiritual attack, when things seem unbearable…look to the hills, God's help is there! I will not try to fight my own battles or solve my own problems.

*Casting all your care upon him; for he careth for you. Be sober, be vigilant; because your adversary the devil, as a roaring lion, walketh about, seeking whom he may devour:*
1 Peter 5:7-8

*I will lift up mine eyes unto the hills, from whence cometh my help. My help cometh from the LORD, which made heaven and earth. He will not suffer thy foot to be moved: he that keepeth thee will not slumber. Behold, he that keepeth Israel shall neither slumber nor sleep. The LORD is thy keeper: the LORD is thy shade upon thy right hand. The sun shall not smite thee by day, nor the moon by night. The LORD shall preserve thee from all evil: he shall preserve thy soul. The LORD shall preserve thy going out and thy coming in from this time forth, and even for evermore.*
Psalm 121:1-8

# God's presence satisfies every need, every desire; God is more than enough!

*And Jesus said unto them, I am the bread of life: he that cometh to me shall never hunger; and he that believeth on me shall never thirst.*
John 6:35

*Reflections -*

**No matter how much people attempt to love – human love has holes and gaps, it's flawed. No matter how good it is, there will always be something lacking, some stress point, some weak place because only the love of God is flawless.**

*Charity suffereth long, and is kind, charity envieth not; charity vaunteth not itself, is not puffed up, Doth not behave itself unseemly, seeketh not her own, is not easily provoked, thinketh no evil; Rejoiceth not in iniquity, but rejoiceth in the truth; Beareth all things, believeth all things, hopeth all things, endureth all things.*
1 Corinthians 13:4-7

*Reflections -*

# Only God is able to do everything well, all the time!

*Great in the LORD, and greatly to be praised; and his greatness is unsearchable. One generation shall praise thy works to another, and shall declare thy mighty acts. I will speak of the glorious honour of thy majesty, and of thy wondrous works. And men shall speak of the might of thy terrible acts: and I will declare thy greatness. They shall abundantly utter the memory of thy great goodness, and shall sing of thy righteousness. The LORD is gracious, and full of compassion; slow to anger, and of great mercy. The LORD is good to all, and his tender mercies are over all his works. All thy works shall praise thee, O LORD; and thy saints shall bless thee.*
*Psalm 145:3-10*

# Lord, You are my source.

*And this is the confidence that we have in him, that, if we ask any thing according to his will, he heareth us: And if we know that he hear us, whatsoever we ask, we know that we have the petitions that we desired of him.*
1 John 5:14-15

# God, I bow only to You!

*For thou shalt worship no other god: for the LORD, whose name is Jealous, is a jealous God:*
Exodus 34:14

**God is so patient with mankind, as we fumble through life, making mistakes and missing the mark. He guides us back into alignment; giving us the opportunity to surrender to His divine will for our lives.**

*For thou, Lord, art good, and ready to forgive; and plenteous in mercy unto all them that call upon thee.*
Psalm 86:5

# Stand still and let God move!

*And Moses said unto the people, Fear ye not, stand still, and see the salvation of the LORD, which he will shew to you to day: for the Egyptians whom ye have seen to day, ye shall see them again no more for ever. The LORD shall fight for you, and ye shall hold your peace.*
Exodus 14:13-14

**Lord, help me to disengage from all weights, distractions, and sins; and focus on dwelling with You!**

*Wherefore seeing we also are compassed about with so great a cloud of witnesses, let us lay aside every weight, and the sin which doth so easily beset us, and let us run with patience the race that is set before us, looking unto Jesus the author and finisher of our faith; who for the joy that was set before him endured the cross, despising the shame, and is set down at the right hand of the throne of God.*
Hebrews 12:1-2

*Reflections -*

**When I ponder God's person, attitude, disposition and His character, I stand in awe of Him. How, I'll never know, I'm just grateful that God is God!**

*Thine, O LORD is the greatness, and the power, and the glory, and the victory, and the majesty: for all that is in the heaven and in the earth is thine; thine is the kingdom, O LORD, and thou art exalted as head above all. Both riches and honour come of thee, and thou reignest over all; and in thine hand is power and might; and in thine hand it is to make great, and to give strength unto all. Now therefore, our God, we thank thee, and praise thy glorious name.*
1 Chronicles 29:11-13

# Lord, I vow my forever to You!

*One thing have I desired of the LORD, that will I seek after; that I may dwell in the house of the LORD all the days of my life, to behold the beauty of the LORD, and to enquire in his temple.*
Psalm 27:4

*Reflections -*

# I am careful as to what I allow my mouth to utter, for it contains life and death.

*Death and life are in the power of the tongue: and they that love it shall eat the fruit thereof.*
Proverbs 18:21

*Reflections -*

# Forgiveness of sin is a gift from God that cannot be rationalized, it must just be accepted.

*If we confess our sins, he is faithful and just to forgive us our sins, and to cleanse us from all unrighteousness.*
1 John 1:9

*Reflections -*

**Human love has boundaries and limits. It can only be pushed so far and endure so much. While human love only has so much to give before it becomes exhausted, God's love is inexhaustible!**

*The LORD hath appeared of old unto me, saying, Yea, I have loved thee with an everlasting love: therefore with lovingkindness have I drawn thee.*
Jeremiah 31:3

*Reflections -*

**God's love is not fueled by a return of love. In other words, God doesn't love us because we love Him. God's love is self-reliant, it depends on itself.**

*Herein is love, not that we loved God, but that he loved us, and sent his Son to be the propitiation for our sins.*
1 John 4:10

*Reflections -*

# God's love is not a behavior, it's His very nature. Not only does God love, God is love!

*And we have known and believed the love that God hath to us. God is love; and he that dwelleth in love dwelleth in God, and God in him.*
1 John 4:16

*Reflections -*

# Faith removes doubt and fear, because it makes tangible that which is intangible.

*Now faith is the substance of things hoped for, the evidence of things not seen.*
Hebrews 11:1

*Reflections -*

# God has equipped me with all that I need for this pilgrimage called life.

*But my God shall supply all your need according to his riches in glory by Christ Jesus.*
Philippians 4:19

*Reflections -*

# Before the foundation of the world, God had a plan for my life!

*According as he hath chosen us in him before the foundation of the world, that we should be holy and without blame before him in love: Having predestinated us unto the adoption of children by Jesus Christ to himself, according to the good pleasure of his will, To the praise of the glory of his grace, wherein he hath made us accepted in the beloved.*
Ephesians 1:4-6

# God is perfect and I love Him for it!

*Be ye therefore perfect, even as your Father which is in heaven is perfect.*
Matthew 5:48

*Reflections -*

**In this world, every question will not be answered and every explanation will not be given. There are some things that will remain a mystery. Only God is all-knowing. And truth be told, only God can handle and manage omniscience. Lord, let my quest for knowledge and understanding always be God-led.**

*Hast thou not known? hast thou not heard, that the everlasting God, the LORD, the Creator of the ends of the earth, fainteth not, neither is weary? there is no searching of his understanding.*
Isaiah 40:28

*O the depth of the riches both of the wisdom and knowledge of God! how unsearchable are his judgments, and his ways past finding out!*
Romans 11:33

*Reflections -*

**The believer is never lost or merely wandering. God provides directions and instructions, even when the destination is unknown. Trust His directions and instructions to get you to your destination on time!**

*The steps of a good man are ordered by the LORD: and he delighteth in his way.*
Psalm 37:23

*For I know the thoughts that I think toward you, saith the LORD, thoughts of peace, and not of evil, to give you an expected end.*
Jeremiah 29:11

*Reflections -*

# Heaven is a place, not an experience!

*In my Father's house are many mansions: if it were not so, I would have told you. I go to prepare a place for you. And if I go and prepare a place for you, I will come again, and receive you unto myself; that where I am, there ye may be also.*
John 14:2-3

*Reflections -*

# It's time for the world to see God in me!

*Ye are the light of the world. A city that is set on an hill cannot be hid. Neither do men light a candle, and put it under a bushel, but on a candlestick; and it giveth light unto all that are in the house. Let your light so shine before men, that they may see your good works, and glorify your Father which is in heaven.*
Matthew 5:14-16

*Reflections -*

# I will sacrifice the appeasement of worldly things to follow Jesus.

*Love not the world, neither the things that are in the world. If any man love the world, the love of the Father is not in him.*
1 John 2:15

*Reflections -*

# God is my satisfying portion!

*The LORD is the portion of mine inheritance and of my cup: thou maintainest my lot. The lines are fallen unto me in pleasant places; yea, I have a goodly heritage.*
Psalm 16:5-6

*Reflections -*

# Only in God do I find life and purpose.

*For in him we live, and move, and have our being; as certain also of your own poets have said, For we are also his offspring.*
Acts 17:28

# Thank You, Lord for setting me free from this world! I made it with Him, to Him, in time!

*Stand fast therefore in the liberty wherewith Christ hath made us free, and be not entangled again with the yoke of bondage.*
Galatians 5:1

*Reflections -*

# God is making wonderful changes in my life!

*Therefore if any man be in Christ, he is a new creature: old things are passed away; behold, all things are become new.*
2 Corinthians 5:17

Learning to live life as God intended is an incredible journey. It's a stress free, worry-free zone…a place where every need is met and every God-ordained prayer is answered…a place where the trials of life lose their power to devastate, but become mere experiences to see and encounter the power of God, learn the wisdom of God and draw ever-so-close to God.

*The steps of a good man are ordered by the LORD: and he delighteth in his way. Though he fall, he shall not be utterly cast down: for the LORD upholdeth him with his hand. I have been young, and now am old; yet have I not seen the righteous forsaken, nor his seed begging bread. He is ever merciful, and lendeth; and his seed is blessed.*
Psalm 37:23-26

*Reflections -*

# I am lost without You,
# but I win with You!

*Now thanks be unto God, which always causeth us to triumph in Christ, and maketh manifest the savour of his knowledge by us in every place.*
2 Corinthians 2:14

*Reflections -*

# Total dependence on God is a good thing. That's where I want to be.

*The LORD is my shepherd; I shall not want. He maketh me to lie down in green pastures: he leadeth me beside the still waters. He restoreth my soul: he leadeth me in the paths of righteousness for his name's sake. Yea, though I walk through the valley of the shadow of death, I will fear no evil: for thou art with me; thy rod and thy staff they comfort me. Thou preparest a table before me in the presence of mine enemies: thou anointest my head with oil; my cup runneth over. Surely goodness and mercy shall follow me all the days of my life: and I will dwell in the house of the LORD for ever.*
Psalm 23:1-6

*Reflections -*

# It is God who gives us the ability to believe in Him.

*For by grace are ye saved through faith; and that not of yourselves: it is the gift of God: Not of works, lest any man should boast.*
Ephesians 2:8-9

*Reflections -*

# In Him, there is movement, and no chaos!

*But grow in grace, and in the knowledge of our Lord and Saviour Jesus Christ. To him be glory both now and for ever. Amen.*
2 Peter 3:18

# Overthinking causes you to waste time and possibly miss your blessings.

*Be careful for nothing; but in every thing by prayer and supplication with thanksgiving let your requests be made known unto God. And the peace of God, which passeth all understanding, shall keep your hearts and minds through Christ Jesus.*
Philippians 4:6-7

*Reflections -*

# God is so amazing!

*For thou art my lamp, O LORD: and the LORD will lighten my darkness. For by thee I have run through a troop: by my God have I leaped over a wall. As for God, his way is perfect; the word of the LORD is tried: he is a buckler to all them that trust in him. For who is God, save the LORD? and who is a rock, save our God? God is my strength and power: and he maketh my way perfect. He maketh my feet like hinds' feet: and setteth me upon my high places. He teacheth my hands to war; so that a bow of steel is broken by mine arms. Thou hast given me the shield of thy salvation: and thy gentleness hath made me great. Thou hast enlarged my steps under me; so that my feet did not slip.*

2 Samuel 22:29-37

# I will go for God!

*Also I heard the voice of the Lord, saying, Whom shall I send,*
*and who will go for us?*
*Then said I, Here am I; send me.*
Isaiah 6:8

*Reflections -*

# God's love is unconditional.

*The LORD hath appeared of old unto me, saying, Yea, I have loved thee with an everlasting love: therefore with lovingkindness have I drawn thee.*
Jeremiah 31:3.

# Don't give your carnal mind access to your mouth!

*For to be carnally minded is death; but to be spiritually minded is life and peace. Because the carnal mind is enmity against God: for it is not subject to the law of God, neither indeed can be.*
Romans 8:6-7

*Set a watch, O LORD, before my mouth; keep the door of my lips.*
Psalm 141:3

*Reflections -*

# You have to learn how to be who God has called you to be.

*Teach me thy way, O LORD; I will walk in thy truth: unite my heart to fear thy name.*
Psalm 86:11

*Make you perfect in every good work to do his will, working in you that which is well-pleasing in his sight, through Jesus Christ; to whom be glory for ever and ever. Amen.*
Hebrews 13:21

# It's all about God, after all, it is His world.

*Let us hear the conclusion of the whole matter: Fear God, and keep his commandments: for this is the whole duty of man. For God shall bring every work into judgment, with every secret thing, whether it be good, or whether it be evil.*
Ecclesiastes 12:13-14

*For by him were all things created, that are in heaven, and that are in earth, visible and invisible, whether they be thrones, or dominions, or principalities, or powers: all things were created by him, and for him; And he is before all things, and by him all things consist.*
Colossians 1:16-17

*Reflections -*

**God gives us Himself, because we need Him. Matriculating successfully through this world without Him is impossible. Without God, humanity is doomed to fail. Life will be unfulfilling, without purpose…full, but empty.**

*I am the vine, ye are the branches: He that abideth in me, and I in him, the same bringeth forth much fruit: for without me ye can do nothing.*
John 15:5

*And I gave my heart to seek and search out by wisdom concerning all things that are done under heaven: this sore travail hath God given to the sons of man to be exercised therewith. I have seen all the works that are done under the sun; and, behold, all is vanity and vexation of spirit.*
Ecclesiastes 1:13-14

# Lord, help me to not be affected by the worldliness around me.

*Now unto him that is able to keep you from falling and to present you faultless before the presence of his glory with exceeding joy,*
Jude 24

# Make your environment conducive for God.

*Be ye not unequally yoked together with unbelievers: for what fellowship hath righteousness with unrighteousness? and what communion hath light with darkness? And what concord hath Christ with Belial? or what part hath he that believeth with an infidel? And what agreement hath the temple of God with idols? for ye are the temple of the living God; as God hath said, I will dwell in them, and walk in them; and I will be their God, and they shall be my people. Wherefore come out from among them, and be ye separate, saith the Lord, and touch not the unclean thing; and I will receive you. And will be a Father unto you, and ye shall be my sons and daughters, saith the Lord Almighty.*
2 Corinthians 6:14-18

*Reflections -*

# God responds to the intensity of our hunger and thirst for righteousness!

*Blessed are they which do hunger and thirst after righteousness:*
*for they shall be filled.*
Matthew 5:6

# It's not just the work, it's the walk.

*Lord, who shall abide in thy tabernacle? who shall dwell in thy holy hill? He that walketh uprightly, and worketh righteousness, and speaketh the truth in his heart.*
Psalm 15:1-2

# Make your choice!

*I call heaven and earth to record this day against you, that I have set before you life and death, blessing and cursing: therefore choose life, that both thou and thy seed may live:*
Deuteronomy 30:19

# Set free? Stay free!

*If the Son therefore shall make you free, ye shall be free indeed.*
John 8:36

*Stand fast therefore in the liberty wherewith Christ hath made*
*us free, and be not entangled again with the yoke of bondage.*
Galatians 5:1

*Reflections -*

# Don't choose to go to hell.

*But the fearful, and unbelieving, and the abominable, and murderers, and whoremongers, and sorcerers, and idolaters, and all liars, shall have their part in the lake which burneth with fire and brimstone: which is the second death.*
Revelation 21:8

*Reflections -*

# God created humanity with a need for Him. Man was not created to exist without relationship with Almighty God!

*I am the true vine, and my Father is the husbandman. Every branch in me that beareth not fruit he taketh away: and every branch that beareth fruit, he purgeth it, that it may bring forth more fruit. Now ye are clean through the word which I have spoken unto you. Abide in me, and I in you. As the branch cannot bear fruit of itself, except it abide in the vine; no more can ye, except ye abide in me. I am the vine, ye are the branches: He that abideth in me, and I in him, the same bringeth forth much fruit: for without me ye can do nothing.*
John 15:1-5

# Almost finished is not finished…finish well!

*Brethren, I count not myself to have apprehended: but this one thing I do, forgetting those things which are behind, and reaching forth unto those things which are before, I press toward the mark for the prize of the high calling of God in Christ Jesus.*
Philippians 3:13-14

**The believer is God's representative in the earth realm. Lord, help me to be a constant reflection of You!**

*Let your light so shine before men, that they may see your good works, and glorify your Father which is in heaven.*
Matthew 5:16

*Reflections -*

# With change comes change.

*This I say therefore, and testify in the Lord, that ye henceforth walk not as other Gentiles walk, in the vanity of their mind, Having the understanding darkened, being alienated from the life of God through the ignorance that is in them, because of the blindness of their heart: Who being past feeling have given themselves over unto lasciviousness, to work all uncleanness with greediness. But ye have not so learned Christ; If so be that ye have heard him, and have been taught by him, as the truth is in Jesus: That ye put off concerning the former conversation the old man, which is corrupt according to the deceitful lusts; And be renewed in the spirit of your mind; And that ye put on the new man, which after God is created in righteousness and true holiness. Wherefore putting away lying, speak every man truth with his neighbour: for we are members one of another. Be ye angry, and sin not: let not the sun go down upon your wrath: Neither give place to the devil. Let him that stole steal no more: but rather let him labour, working with his hands the thing which is good, that he may have to give to him that needeth. Let no corrupt communication proceed out of your mouth, but that which is good to the use of edifying, that it may minister grace unto the hearers. And grieve not the holy Spirit of God, whereby ye are sealed unto the day of redemption. Let all bitterness, and wrath, and anger, and clamour, and evil speaking, be put away from you, with all malice: And be ye kind one to another, tenderhearted, forgiving one another, even as God for Christ's sake hath forgiven you.*
Ephesians 4:17-32

*Reflections -*

# God declares, "I am God." Yes Lord, You are God!

*Be still, and know that I am God: I will be exalted among the heathen, I will be exalted in the earth.*
Psalm 46:10

*Reflections -*

# God never losses!

*These things I have spoken unto you, that in me ye might have peace. In the world ye shall have tribulation: but be of good cheer; I have overcome the world.*
John 16:33

*Reflections -*

**God is ever-present – He is already present in the spaces and times that we are yet to occupy. God is already present in every tomorrow, throughout eternity.**

*O LORD, thou hast searched me, and known me. Thou knowest my down-sitting and mine uprising, thou understandest my thought afar off. Thou compassest my path and my lying down, and art acquainted with all my ways. Whither shall I go from thy spirit? or whither shall I flee from thy presence? If I ascend up into heaven, thou art there: if I make my bed in hell, behold, thou art there. If I take the wings of the morning, and dwell in the uttermost parts of the sea; Even there shall thy hand lead me, and thy right hand shall hold me. If I say, Surely the darkness shall cover me; even the night shall be light about me. Yea, the darkness hideth not from thee; but the night shineth as the day: the darkness and the light are both alike to thee.*
Psalm 139:1-3, 7-12

*The eyes of the LORD are in every place, beholding the evil and the good.*
Proverbs 15:3

# With surrender, comes sacrifice!

*I BESEECH you therefore, brethren, by the mercies of God, that ye present your bodies a living sacrifice, holy, acceptable unto God, which is your reasonable service. And be not conformed to this world: but be ye transformed by the renewing of your mind, that ye may prove what is that good, and acceptable, and perfect, will of God. For I say, through the grace given unto me, to every man that is among you, not to think of himself more highly than he ought to think; but to think soberly, according as God hath dealt to every man the measure of faith*
Romans 12:1-3

# Until the only life they
# see in me is You!

*I am crucified with Christ: nevertheless I live; yet not I, but Christ liveth in me: and the life which I now live in the flesh I live by the faith of the Son of God, who loved me, and gave himself for me.*
Galatians 2:20

*Reflections -*

# No pressure, just opportunity!

*Behold, I stand at the door, and knock: if any man hear my voice, and open the door, I will come in to him, and will sup with him, and he with me. To him that overcometh will I grant to sit with me in my throne, even as I also overcame, and am set down with my Father in his throne.*
Revelation 3:20-21

# God requires our undivided attention!

*Then said Jesus unto his disciples, If any man will come after me, let him deny himself, and take up his cross, and follow me. For whosoever will save his life shall lose it: and whosoever will lose his life for my sake shall find it.*
Matthew 16:24-25

Reflections -

# He didn't replace me; He gave me another chance!

*Who is a God like unto thee, that pardoneth iniquity, and passeth by the transgression of the remnant of his heritage? he retaineth not his anger for ever, because he delighteth in mercy. He will turn again, he will have compassion upon us; he will subdue our iniquities; and thou wilt cast all their sins into the depths of the sea.*
Micah 7:18-19


*If we confess our sins, he is faithful and just to forgive us our sins, and to cleanse us from all unrighteousness.*
1 John 1:9


*My little children, these things write I unto you, that ye sin not. And if any man sin, we have an advocate with the Father, Jesus Christ the righteous: And he is the propitiation for our sins: and not for ours only, but also for the sins of the whole world.*
1 John 2:1-2

*Reflections -*

# Prayer and fasting are the keys that open the locks of our deep-seated sins.

*Howbeit this kind goeth not out but by prayer and fasting.*
Matthew 17:21

*Reflections -*

# How can I truly be satisfied by someone that I fail to get to know?

*Take my yoke upon you, and learn of me; for I am meek and lowly in heart: and ye shall find rest unto your souls.*
Matthew 11:29

*Reflections -*

# There is often pain with recovery.

*For our light affliction, which is but for a moment, worketh for*
*us a far more exceeding and eternal weight of glory;*
2 Corinthians 4:17

*Reflections -*

# Stop giving God the relationship that you give everyone else you have relationship with.

*And thou shalt love the Lord thy God with all thy heart, and with all thy soul, and with all thy mind, and with all thy strength: this is the first commandment.*
Mark 12:30

*Reflections -*

# Situations come to challenge your faith, not your God.

*Jesus said unto him, If thou canst believe, all things are possible to him that believeth.*
Mark 9:23

*I can do all things through Christ which strengtheneth me.*
Philippians 4:13

# You can't really help anyone, until God helps you!

*And why beholdest thou the mote that is in thy brother's eye, but considerest not the beam that is in thine own eye? Or how wilt thou say to thy brother, Let me pull out the mote out of thine eye; and, behold, a beam is in thine own eye? Thou hypocrite, first cast out the beam out of thine own eye; and then shalt thou see clearly to cast out the mote out of thy brother's eye.*
Matthew 7:3-5

*Reflections -*

# In order to learn, you have to be open.

*Blessed are they which do hunger and thirst after righteousness:
for they shall be filled.*
Matthew 5:6

# God's plan is never off schedule, His timing is perfect!

*To every thing there is a season, and a time to every purpose under the heaven: …He hath made every thing beautiful in his time: also he hath set the world in their heart, so that no man can find out the work that God maketh from the beginning to the end.*
Ecclesiastes 3:1,11

*I had fainted, unless I had believed to see the goodness of the LORD in the land of the living. Wait on the LORD: be of good courage, and he shall strengthen thine heart: wait I say, on the LORD.*
Psalm 27:13-14

**So often we ask the Lord to use us for His glory and when He does, we fret and resist Him. Lord, help us. Lord help us, in Jesus' name!**

*Beloved, think it not strange concerning the fiery trial which is to try you, as though some strange thing happened unto you: But rejoice, inasmuch as ye are partakers of Christ's sufferings; that, when his glory shall be revealed, ye may be glad also with exceeding joy.*
1 Peter 4:12-13

*Reflections -*

# Lord God, work on me until You are finished and You are satisfied....until every thought is Yours.....every word is Yours.....and every action is Yours!

*Search me, O God, and know my heart: try me, and know my thoughts: And see if there be any wicked way in me, and lead me in the way everlasting.*
Psalm 139:23-24


*But we all, with open face beholding as in a glass the glory of the Lord, are changed into the same image from glory to glory, even as by the Spirit of the Lord.*
2 Corinthians 3:18

# About the Author

Karen Rutherford is a pastor, teacher, inspirational speaker, singer and most importantly, a devoted, Spirit-filled, disciple of Jesus Christ. Pastor Rutherford ministers a message of God's love and grace through relationship with Jesus Christ. Her love and passion for God and the Gospel has inspired many to deepen their walk with the Lord. Being a survivor of life's many storms, she has a special gift to encourage others to gather their broken pieces and live, as God forgives and forgets through the blood of His Son, Jesus Christ. She currently serves as the senior pastor of Greater Washington Deliverance Temple, in Laurel, Maryland.